AF428111

MAN'S FURRY BEST FRIEND ALL ABOUT DOGS

Animal Book for Toddlers | Children's Animal Books

Speedy Publishing LLC

40 E. Main St. #1156

Newark, DE 19711

www.speedypublishing.com

Copyright 2017

All Rights reserved. No part of this book may be reproduced or used in any way or form or by any means whether electronic or mechanical, this means that you cannot record or photocopy any material ideas or tips that are provided in this book.

One of the most popular pets around the world is the dog. They have played a key role in our lives for a long time, maybe even thousands of years. Often, they are referred to as Man's Best Friend since they have the ability to assist mankind in multiple ways. Over 30% of U.S. families enjoy having them as pets. It has been shown that having a pet dog around makes people healthier. They have less heart attacks and live longer. Read further to learn about different breeds of dogs and enjoying them as a pet.

DIFFERENT BREEDS AND TYPES

There are many different breeds and types of dogs which can vary in size from being only a couple of inches tall up to about three feet tall. Some breeds are considered to be better for outdoor or indoor pets and some breeds are known as working dogs. Some of the jobs that they can perform include police work, hunting, rescue work, and there are even seeing-eye dogs to assist the blind. Since they are very intelligent and are willing to be trained, they make a terrific work animal or a great companion.

Beagle

Dogs are considered to be mammals. While the different breeds have different skills and characteristics, most of them have strong muscles, large teeth, they walk on their toes, and they can run fast and jump. They are also warm-blooded, produce milk for feeding their babies, and have hair for fur. Humans are also considered to be mammals as well as horses, elephants and whales.

Pug

THEIR AMAZING SENSES OF
SMELL, SIGHT AND HEARING

K-9
POLICE DOG

SMELL

Their excellent sense of smell makes them good at tracking and sniffing out drugs, bombs, and other illegal items. There are even some that are bred particularly to boost this sense. Their sense of smell is about 100,000 times greater than a human's.

Research has found it to be likely that they have the ability to smell anxiety, fear and sadness. Adrenaline, the flight-or-fight hormone, which is undetectable by our sense of smell, apparently can be sensed by a dog's sense of smell. Additionally, anxiety or fear is often accompanied by an increase in blood flow and heart rate, which then sends any telltale body chemicals to the surface of the skin. While attempting to cover up your feeling with a slight smile might just fool your friends, it will not fool your best friends.

Siberian Huskies

VISION

They also have an excellent vision field which allows them to see in almost a complete circle. Contrary to popular belief, they don't see the world around them as black and white. Actually, their vision is similar to humans that have red and green color blindness.

HEARING

Their hearing is highly sensitive and has a tremendous range of frequency which enables them to hear sounds that we as humans might not be able to hear. It has been shown that they are able to locate a sound's source within approximately six-hundredths of one second. Since their ears are so mobile, they can capture the sound and funnel it to the eardrum.

French Bulldog

German Shepherd

You may see your dog raise one ear to capture the first sound, and will then raise both ears to obtain the maximum number of the sound waves. Along with their sense of smell this makes them great for guarding and protecting since they can detect intruders, often from a great distance.

PETS

They can be a terrific pet for children. The key is training both the dog as well as the child. Children need to learn how to treat the dog so that it will not retaliate. There are expert trainers that can help you with choosing the right dog and training your dog and kids how to behave around each other.

SELECTING A DOG

There are terrific breeds to choose from, but keep in mind that each breed is different. If you are selecting a dog to be a pet, you should choose one that agrees with your lifestyle. Here are a few questions to ask yourself before getting a dog:

Are you active? You need to be honest with the answer to this question since some like to simply lay around and others need a lot of exercise. Select a breed that fits your activity level.

House or yard dog? Some enjoy being inside, but some breeds like to be outside. Be sure to select one that will enjoy the home and yard that you have.

Are children a part of your family? Be sure to investigate whether or not the breed you want is good with children.

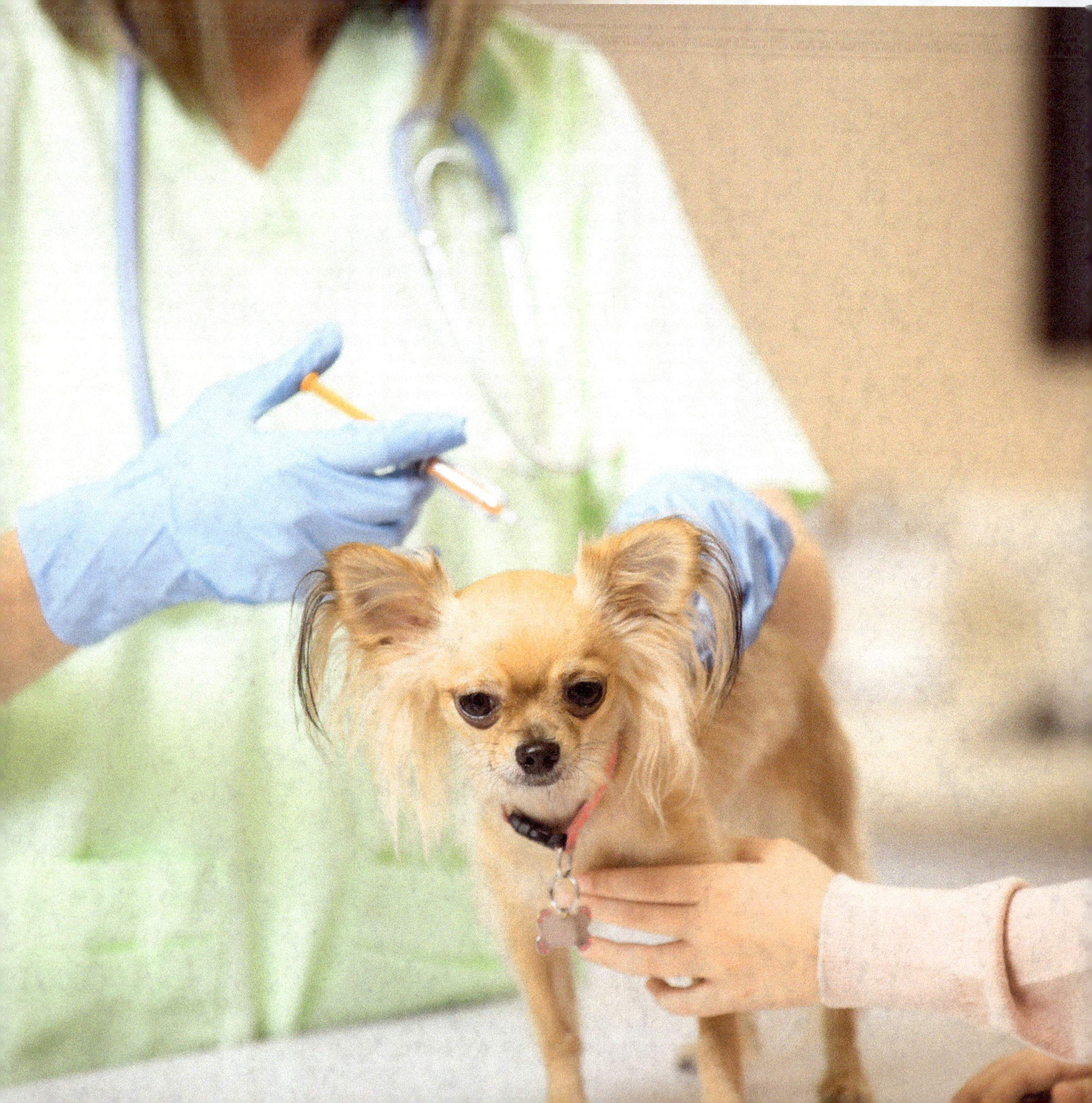

Are you financially able to afford a dog? Prior to getting a dog, be sure to consider the amount of money that is involved with having a dog. Some of these costs include feeding it, maintaining its shots, vet visits, illnesses, just to name a few.

Do you have time for a dog? They need physical and emotional support which can take up a lot of your time. Make sure you have considered this prior to getting one.

Be sure to take your time and do your homework before deciding on getting a dog so that you will be able to enjoy its friendship and comfort for many years.

MOVIES ABOUT DOGS

There are many dog movies and kids love them. Some of the more popular movies are 101 Dalmatians, 102 Dalmatians, Air Bud, All Dogs Go to Heaven, Aussie and Ted's Great Adventure, Because of Winn-Dixie, Beethoven, Call of the Wild, Cats and Dogs, Eight Below, Homeward Bound, Lady and the Tramp, My Dog Skip, Snow Dogs and The Shaggy Dog.

Dalmatians

You do not need to be a dog lover to enjoy any of these movies. However, some of the movies about dogs are rated PG, so kids, please check with your parents before watching any of these movies.

POLICE DOGS

Police dogs are used in assisting police with solving crimes and during the past several years have become a key part of law enforcement. They have saved lives using their unique skills and their bravery. They are watchful, loyal, and protective of the police officer and often are considered to be an important and irreplaceable part of police agencies.

Police Dogs

Dog Training

POLICE DOG EXPERTS

Today, police dogs are trained in a specific area. You might call them an expert in their field. Listed below are a few of the specific dog roles in a police agency:

TRACKING: Police dogs that specialize in tracking use their tremendous sense of smell for tracking missing persons or criminal suspects. They are trained for years and have the ability to find even the most cunning suspect. Many suspects would be able to elude the police without these dogs.

SUBSTANCE DETECTORS: This type of expert police dog uses their sense of smell to assist the police, but not in the same way that a tracking dog does. The substance dogs focus on finding a certain substance. Some specialize in identifying explosives or bombs.

Not only are these courageous dogs trained in detecting an explosive, but they are also trained in how to respond and safely alert their officer to the location of the explosive. Other dogs might focus strictly on illegal drugs. They save the officers from having to search by hand through a car or luggage since they are able to determine by their sense of smell if there is an illegal substance present.

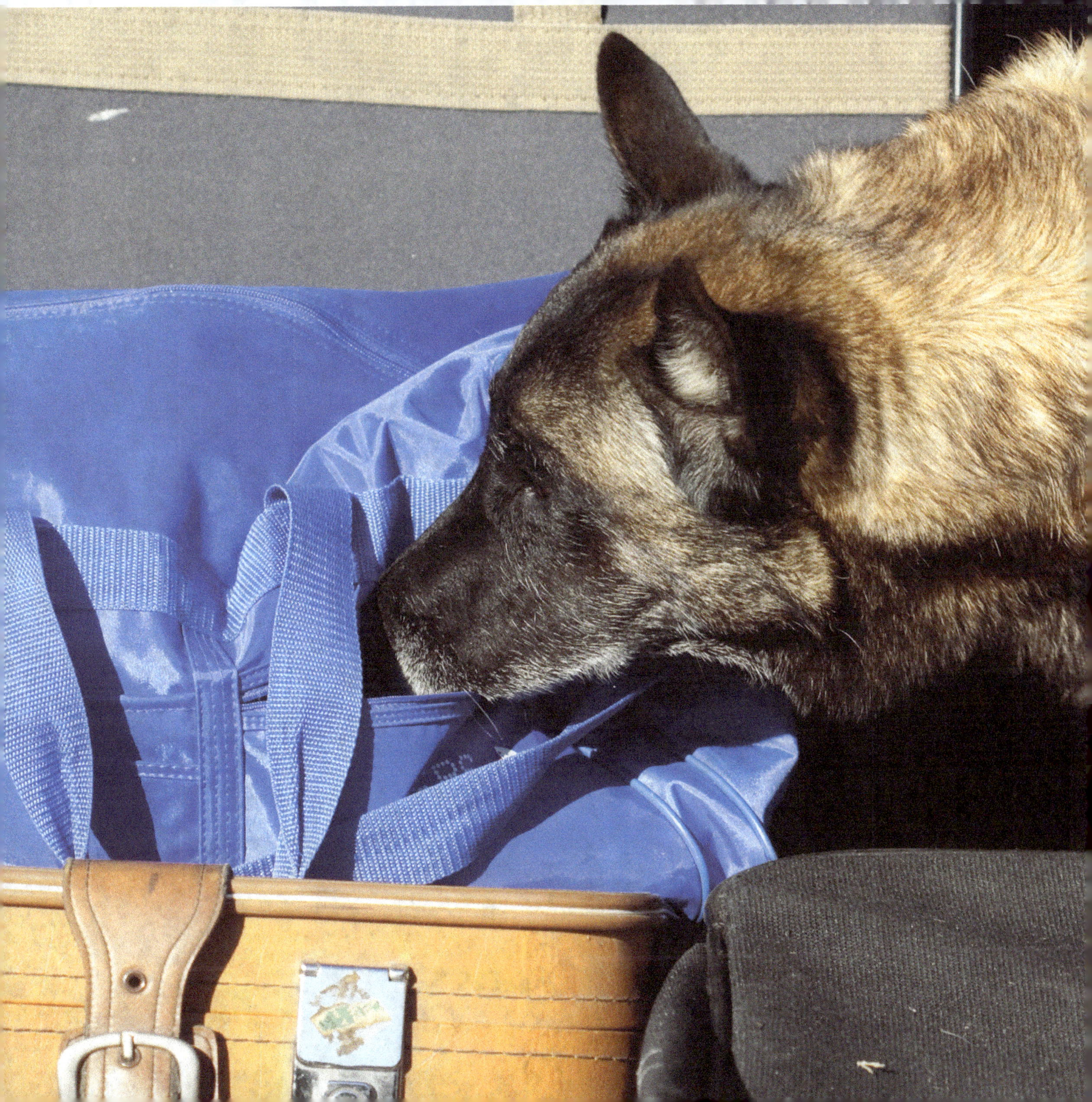

PUBLIC ENFORCEMENT: Public enforcement police dogs assist the police officers in keeping order. They might chase a criminal and hold them until the police officer arrives, or they might simply guard an area such as a prison or a jail to keep criminals from escaping.

CADAVER DOGS: While it might seem somewhat gross, cadaver dogs are trained to find dead bodies, which is a key function within the agency and these dogs are good at what they do.

035
EMERGENCY
9-1-1
P

Poodle

WOULD MY POODLE BE A GOOD CANDIDATE?

While your poodle might be a terrific dog, it probably isn't going to be a good fit as a police dog, which needs to have very specific and special training. There are several different dog breeds that can be trained for police work. The breed often will depend upon what type of work they will be doing.

Some of the more popular breeds include German Shepherds and Belgian Malinois, even though other breeds such as Beagles and Bloodhounds are good candidates in some cases. No matter what breed it is, these dogs are typically trained as puppies in learning their new job.

Belgian Malinois

POLICE DOG RETIREMENT

These dogs are typically treated as heroes. In many instances, they will go live with the police officer they were partnered with. They have already spent several years with that person and see them as family, and this works out for both the dog and the officer.

For additional about dogs and the different breeds of dogs you can go to your local library, research the internet, and ask questions of your teachers, family and friends.

Visit
BABY PROFESSOR
EDUCATION KIDS
www.BabyProfessorBooks.com
to download Free Baby Professor eBooks
and view our catalog of new and exciting
Children's Books

www.ingramcontent.com/pod-product-compliance
Lightning Source LLC
Chambersburg PA
CBHW060224120726
48009CB00003B/141